GREEN CRAFTS
for children

GREEN CRAFTS
for children

35 step-by-step projects using natural, recycled and found materials

Emma Hardy

CICO BOOKS
LONDON NEW YORK

NEWCASTLE REGION
LIBRARY

-- SEP 2008

For our good friends Clem and Luca with lots of love

Published in 2008 by CICO Books
an imprint of Ryland Peters & Small
20–21 Jockey's Fields, London WC1R 4BW

www.cicobooks.co.uk

10 9 8 7 6 5 4 3 2 1

Text copyright © Emma Hardy 2008
Design and photography copyright © CICO Books 2008

The author's moral rights have been asserted. All rights
reserved. No part of this publication may be reproduced,
stored in a retrieval system, or transmitted in any form or
by any means, electronic, mechanical, photocopying, or
otherwise, without the prior permission of the publisher.

A CIP catalogue record for this book is available from the
British Library.

ISBN-13: 978 1 906094 74 4

Printed in China

Editor: Robin Gurdon
Designer: Liz Sephton
Photographer: Debbie Patterson

CONTENTS

INTRODUCTION

Children love to make things. Supply them with the materials and they will have hours of fun designing and creating all sorts of wonderful projects. The idea of this book is to encourage creativity and imagination using natural, reclaimed and recycled materials.

In a time where computer games and television can often be the main features of children's leisure time, crafting can provide the perfect antidote, encouraging creativity as well as improving dexterity and patience. Green crafting can encourage children to step outdoors, to look around them and show an interest in their surroundings. Using natural materials can also help to raise an awareness of ecological issues – kids can learn that it is fun to recycle and be aware of their environment.

Collecting things can be great fun especially when the 'finds' can be used to create something else. Encourage children to keep their eyes peeled while on walks in the countryside and beach and even in the garden and house for things that could be used in another way. The projects use a wide range of different techniques from traditional crafts, such as salt dough, French knitting and papier maché, to contemporary ideas like eggshell mosaic and recycled makes.

There are easy to follow step-by-step instructions alongside each project and a list of the materials needed to help make each one, but feel free to improvise with materials that you have available to you.

The projects range from fairly simple ones suitable for very young children, to slightly more complex ones for older kids. However, many of the more difficult projects will be suitable for younger hands with a little assistance.

Children can use the ideas they enjoy using in this book for inspiration to create their own craft projects, which will in turn encourage confidence in their own abilities and ideas. Allow your kids to express themselves and remember that it is very much the pleasure gained from making things that counts. Crafting should be fun, so don't worry about making a mess or the end result being 'perfect'. Just encourage your children to enjoy the process and be proud of their creations!

MATERIALS AND BASIC TECHNIQUES

To get crafting you will need to gather some materials, so here are a few ideas of things to horde. Most of the materials are available for free, either by collecting from nature, recycling or reusing, but here are a few things that are worth buying from an art or stationery shop to get you started.

GLUE

There are lots of different kinds of glue available but you will only need two types for the projects in this book. PVA (left) is a versatile glue that will stick lots of different materials together. It is non-toxic and easy to use, though it can be a little messy so make sure that you cover your work surface with newspaper before you start. Glue sticks are good for sticking paper together but are less effective on bigger items.

PAINT

Poster paints are available in a wide range of colours and are non-toxic and washable (very useful!). For a basic kit, buy red, yellow and blue, which can be mixed together to create lots more colours, and white and black to lighten and darken them. A selection of paintbrushes in different sizes will be useful, but don't spend a lot of money on them. Cheap ones will be fine. Paper plates are very useful for mixing paints on, or use old yoghurt pots for paint and glue.

SCISSORS

Always use safety scissors (far right) when crafting. If you need to cut thicker card, ask an adult to help. Pinking shears (right) are scissors that cut with a jagged edge and are useful when cutting fabric as they will help to stop the edges fraying as well as creating a pretty edge. There are also lots of shaped scissors available from art shops that are great for cutting fancy edges on paper or card.

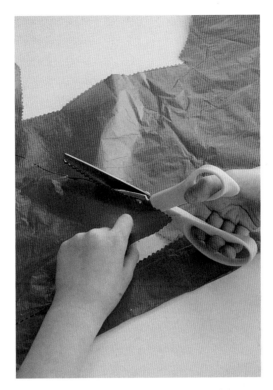

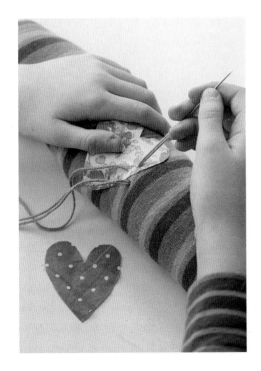

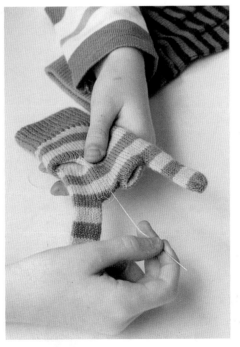

NEEDLES AND THREAD

A basic sewing kit is always handy to have. A few different sizes of needles and cotton thread in a few different colours will all be useful. Embroidery thread and thin wool are good for sewing simple stitches for little fingers as they tend not to knot quite as much as cotton thread.

SEWING

To start sewing, thread the needle with thread or thin wool. Either tie a knot in the end of the thread before you stitch through the fabrics that you are using, pulling the knot right up to the fabric, or make a few stitches at one spot on the wrong side of the fabric and bring the needle through to the right side to begin sewing. Knot or sew a few stitches to secure the thread when you have finished sewing.

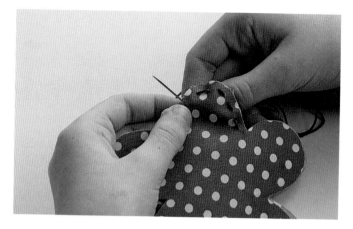

THE RUNNING STITCH

This is the easiest stitch and is can be used for all the projects that require things to be sewn together. It is done by pushing the needle through the fabric from right to left, working in and out through the fabric.

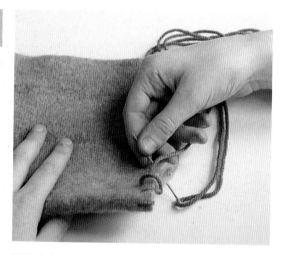

THE WHIPSTITCH

This stitch can be used for the felted bag project and sausage dog. Tie a knot in the end of the thread and stitch though the fabric. Pass the needle from the back of the fabrics though to the front. Bring the needle over the top and through the back to the front again.

SEWING BUTTONS

Make a few stitches through the fabric where you would like to place the button to hold the thread in place. With the needle on the right side of the fabric pass the needle through one of the holes on the button from the back to the front. Push the needle down through the other hole and down through the fabric. Repeat this 5 or 6 times. Make a few stitches underneath the button or on the wrong side of the fabric to finish and cut the thread.

THINGS TO COLLECT

NEWSPAPER

Great for papier-maché projects and essential for covering the work surfaces while you craft. The paper needs to be torn into pieces for papier maché. Because of the fibres in the paper you will find that it will tear much more easily in one direction than another. Rip the paper and if it does not tear in a fairly straight line, turn the paper round and try in the other direction.

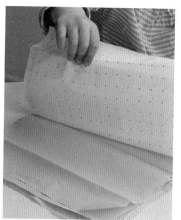

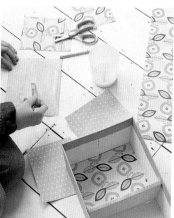

PAPER

Keep old wrapping papers and gift wraps as they often come in great patterns and colours. Tissue paper (above right) is often used to wrap things in shops, and again comes in lots or brilliant colours. Old magazines and comics (above left) are very useful, too. Don't forget to recycle any scraps that you have left over rather than put them in the bin.

BOXES

You can never have too many cardboard boxes as they can be used for so many different creations. Shoeboxes, cereal packets and other food boxes and just about any other cardboard packaging will be useful. Look for different sizes and colours to use.

FABRICS, RIBBONS AND BUTTONS

Collect scraps of fabrics and ribbons that can be useful for lots of projects. Re-use old clothes, including gloves, tights and socks, and cut them up and make them into lots of different things. Old T-shirts and jumpers are worth keeping, too. Buttons make great eyes on hand-crafted toys, so start collecting them in an old jam jar so that you have a selection to choose from.

 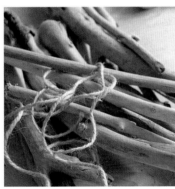

NATURAL COLLECTIONS

Pinecones, seed heads, twigs, leaves, pebbles and driftwood and anything else that you can find on countryside walks or while beachcombing can be used for crafting. Look at the shapes and colours and create all sorts of wonderful makes. Check with an adult before taking things, and never pick berries (unless you know what they are) or mushrooms, which can often be poisonous.

FOOD

Pumpkins, squash and gourds are great for making foodie creatures as are lots of different vegetables and fruits. Flour and salt make wonderful doughs to model with, or just play with, and are very cheap to buy. Nutshells are very useful, too. Potatoes and apples are perfect for printing, as are pears and carrots, which can be used to make lots of different patterns. Dried peas and lentils are good for fillings.

SALT DOUGH

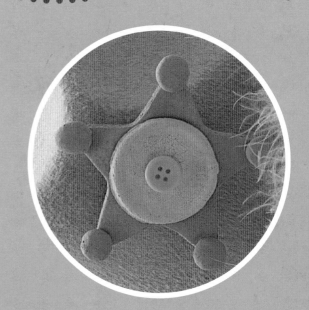

1 SALT-DOUGH LETTERS

These colourful letters made with alphabet cutters are so simple to make. Made with salt dough which, when baked, becomes hard and can be painted, they are quick and inexpensive to make. Glue small magnets onto the back of the letters so that they can be fixed to the fridge, or spell out a name and stick onto a bedroom door.

Materials

- 300g (10oz) plain flour
- 300g (10oz) salt
- 200ml (⅓ pint) lukewarm water
- 1 tablespoon vegetable oil
- Water-based paints and paintbrushes
- Mixing bowl and wooden spoon
- Measuring jug
- Rolling pin and alphabet pastry cutters
- Non-stick baking tray

1 Put 300g of salt into the mixing bowl, pour in the water and mix thoroughly until all the salt is dissolved – doing this before adding the flour will help to create a smoother dough than if it is added at the same time.

2 Add 300g of flour to the bowl, also pour in the vegetable oil at this time. Stir until the mixture becomes stiff, then knead it with your hands to form a firm dough. Scrape the bowl clean and make the dough into a ball.

3 Sprinkle flour onto the work surface and place the ball of dough onto it. Roll the dough out with a rolling pin to an even thickness of about 1cm (½in.).

4 Cut out letters using the cutters and place them onto the tray. Put them in an oven at 100°C (210°F, gas 4) for one hour. When hard turn the oven off but leave them inside to cool to help stop the salt dough from cracking.

5 Use water-soluble paints and a brush to paint the letters in a variety of bright colours, using whatever colour combinations you think works best. When the base coat is dry add decorations in another colour.

SALT-DOUGH LETTERS

2 SALT-DOUGH TEA SET

Salt dough is so simple to make and very easy to mould. Here it has been used to make a cute tea set, perfect for a teddy bear's tea party. Solid shapes made from salt dough like the tea pot, need to be baked in the oven on a very low heat as they can crack if the temperature is too high.

Materials
- Salt dough ingredients (see page 17)
- Pastry cutter
- Rolling pin
- Baking tray
- Paint and brushes

1 Make the dough following the instructions on page 17. Knead it into a smooth dough, collecting all the bits in the bowl into one big lump.

2 Take a piece of dough and put onto a floured surface. Roll it out using the rolling pin to a thickness of about 5mm.

3 Using the pastry cutter cut out some circles for plates and saucers and put onto a baking tray. Make 4 in total.

4 Take a piece of dough and form into a ball to make the teapot. Make 2 small balls with dough and flatten them to make the base and the lid. Make a small handle using a small sausage of dough and a spout shape, and stick all the pieces together to make the teapot. Use a little water to stick them together if they are a little dry. Put onto the baking tray.

5 Take a piece of dough and form into a cup shape, pressing your fingers down in the centre of it to make the right shape. Add a small dough handle made from a sausage-shaped piece of dough and put onto the baking sheet. Make into cups. Make a smaller cup shape and turn it into a jug shape, and put onto the baking sheet.

6 Make a small pot in the same manner as the cup to make a sugar bowl, flattening a small ball of dough to make a lid, finishing with a tiny ball of dough on the top to make a handle.

7 Bake all the pieces in the oven on the lowest setting for about 1 to 1½ hours. Leave them in longer if they are still slightly soft. When all the pieces are completely cool, paint them all white and leave them to dry.

8 Using coloured paints and a fine paintbrush, paint a line around all the plates and saucers adding dots all the way round. Paint flowers onto all the pieces, with thin blue lines round the edges. Leave to dry thoroughly before playing with them.

3 SALT-DOUGH BEADS

This is a great project for very young children to master as the bead shapes are very simple. Make them in different shapes and sizes, bake them and paint them in lovely bright colours, decorating them with patterns or leaving them plain. Bead necklaces are fun to wear, too, and great to give as gifts.

Materials
- Salt dough ingredients (see page 17)
- Baking sheet
- Stick or skewer
- Paints and brushes
- Wool
- Needle

1 Make up the dough, mixing it until it has a soft, pliable texture (see page 17).

2 Place the dough on a flat surface, cover it in flour and knead until smooth.

3 Make bead shapes. Vary the sizes of the beads and push a stick or skewer through to make a hole. Make the hole slightly bigger than you need as it will shrink a little when the salt dough is baked. Make small square beads, again making a hole through the middle. Squash some of the round beads slightly to flatten them. Lay onto a baking tray and bake in the oven at the lowest heat for about 1½ hours.

4 When the beads have cooled completely, paint them in bright colours and leave to dry.

5 Decorate the beads with spots, flowers and patterns in contrasting colours and again leave to dry.

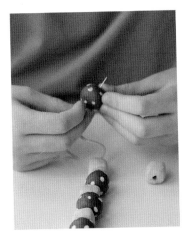

6 Cut a length of wool that is long enough to fit over your head and round your neck, adding extra for the knot. Thread the needle with the wool and thread through the beads in a nice arrangement. Take the needle off the wool and tie the ends of the necklace with a double knot.

4 MAKING PLAY DOUGH

Make great play dough at home using simple ingredients from your Mum's store cupboard. Add food colouring – the brighter the better! – to make it really zingy, and have hours of fun creating all sorts of models and shapes. Raid the kitchen cupboard again for dried pasta, great for sticking in the dough to form faces and patterns. The dough will keep well in an air-tight container.

● ● ● ● ● ● ● ● ● ● ● ● ● ● ●

Materials
- 1 cup of plain flour
- ½ cup of salt
- 2 tablespoons cream of tartar
- 1 tablespoon vegetable oil
- 1 cup water
- Food colouring
- Pan and mixing spoon

1 Put a large cup of plain flour and half a cup of salt into a medium-sized pan.

2 Next add 2 spoonfuls of cream of tartar and 1 spoonful of vegetable oil.

3 Add a few drops of food colouring to a large cup of water and then pour the mixture into the pan.

4 Mix the ingredients together thoroughly and, with the help of an adult, heat the pan gently on a stove until a dough forms.

5 Let the dough cool completely in the pan. Scrape all the bits of dough from around the pan and begin to form it into a lump.

6 Now you can start creating models with the play dough! Dried pasta is great for sticking into the dough to make patterns, shapes and faces.

5 SALT-DOUGH FRUIT

Take inspiration from your own fruit bowl or visit a market to see the huge variety of shapes and colours of the fruits on offer, then mould your salt dough, bake and paint it to create delicious looking ornaments that look good enough to eat. Display them in a bowl and see if they fool your friends. Don't let them eat your dough creations, though, they will taste a bit salty!

Materials
- Salt dough ingredients (see page 17)
- Baking sheet
- Paints and paint brushes
- Green and brown pipe cleaners
- Green felt

1 Measure out the flour, salt and oil and place in a bowl (see page 17). Pour the water in and mix with your hands to form a firm dough. Add more water if necessary, or more flour if the dough is too sticky.

2 Take a piece of dough and form it into a strawberry shape. Make cherries from balls of dough and make a slight hole in the top of them so that the pipe cleaner stalks can be pushed in place when the fruits have been baked. Take a larger piece of dough and make a slice of watermelon and smaller pieces to make the orange segments. Grapes are made from small balls of dough. Put all of the fruits onto a baking tray and bake in the oven for about 1½ hours.

3 When the shapes are all completely cool, they are ready to paint. Paint the strawberries red, the orange segments orange, the grapes pale green, the cherries dark red and the watermelon green on the outside and red in the middle.

4 When the base coats are dry, paint small blobs of yellow all over the strawberries to look like seeds. Leave to dry.

5 Use black paint to add the seeds onto the red part of the watermelon.

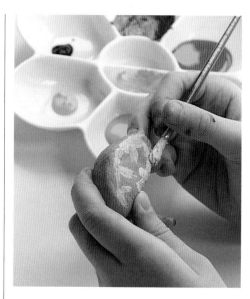

6 Make a lighter shade of orange by mixing in some white paint and use to paint lines onto the orange segments.

7 Cut out the leaves from green felt (using the templates on page 124). Cut a length of green pipe cleaner and bend it in half. Glue each end into the cherries then place a spot of glue on a leaf shape and glue it onto the cherry stalks.

8 Glue another leaf onto the strawberry. When all the pieces are dry, you can paint them with a covering of PVA glue to make them slightly shiny and protect their surfaces from chipping.

6 SALT-DOUGH BROOCH

Cookie cutters are great for making shapes with salt dough. Use a star to make a sheriff's badge, adding little balls of dough at the points for a truly wild-west feel, or try flower shapes stuck on to circle of dough for a pretty brooch. Paint them and decorate with a button or bead, gluing a safety pin to the back.

Materials
- Salt dough ingredients (see page 17)
- Bowl and spoon
- Baking tray
- Rolling pin
- Cutters
- PVA glue
- Paints and brushes
- Buttons
- Scraps of fabric
- Safety pins

1 Put the flour, salt, oil and water into the bowl (see page 17). Mix to form a firm dough. Add more water if the dough is too dry and more flour if it is too sticky. Form the dough into a ball.

2 Sprinkle some flour onto the work surface and roll out to a thickness of about 5mm using the rolling pin. Sprinkle flour onto the dough to prevent it getting too sticky.

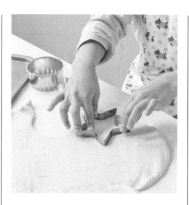

3 Using the cutters, cut out star shapes and make small circles for the sheriff's badges. Put small blobs of dough onto the points of the stars. Cut a large plain circle, a wavy-edged circle and a flower circle for the brooches.

4 Lay them onto a baking sheet and bake in the oven on the lowest setting for about an hour until they are completely hard.

5 When the pieces have all cooled completely, paint them in bright colours and leave to dry.

6 Using the PVA glue, stick the 3 parts of the brooches together and stick small circles onto the middle of the stars.

SALT DOUGH

7 Glue a button onto the middle of the flower brooches and sheriff's badges and leave them to dry.

8 Cut a small piece of fabric and thread through a safety pin. Glue the fabric onto the back of the badges and brooches and leave until the glue is completely set. If you want to give your badges and brooches a shiny look paint them with PVA glue.

PAPIER MACHÉ AND PAPER

7 NATURAL INKS

Picking fruits from the hedgerows is a really fun autumn activity. Why not try making these natural inks with some of your harvest? Add vinegar to the juice to help the ink to keep its colour and a little salt to prevent it going off too quickly. Alternatively, if these ingredients are not available and you are out in the countryside, just squash the berries using whatever you can find (stones would work well), collect the juice in a bucket and write or draw with it. Look for feathers to make into quills.

PAPIER MACHÉ AND PAPER

Materials
- Raspberries
- Blackberries
- Vinegar
- Sieve
- Spoon
- Water
- Salt
- Little jars
- Feather

1 Measure ½ cup of berries and put them in a sieve. Squash the berries with the back of a spoon, collecting the juice that is squeezed out in a bowl underneath.

2 Add ½ a tablespoon of salt to the juice, which will act as a preservative.

3 Add ½ a tablespoon of vinegar to the mixture to help retain the colour. Mix well and pour into a small jar.

4 Dip a feather into the ink and write with it, filling it with ink after writing every two or three letters.

To make invisible ink, simply squeeze a lemon and write with it using the feather or a paintbrush. To reveal the secret message, mix baking soda with equal parts water and brush over the paper or brush grape juice over the paper. Keep this information away from your enemies!

8 PAPIER-MACHÉ BOWL

Making papier maché gives you the perfect opportunity to get your hands covered in goo! Torn strips of newspaper are dipped in glue and then layered onto a mould, like the bowl that we have used here, which can then be painted and decorated when dry. Protect your work surface with old newspaper as this is a lovely, messy project and glue will get everywhere!

Materials
- Bowl
- Petroleum jelly
- Cling film
- PVA glue, bowl and water
- Newspaper
- Paint and brush
- Scraps of wrapping paper

1 Cover the underside of a plastic bowl from the kitchen with a layer of petroleum jelly and a piece of cling film.

2 Tear some sheets of newspaper into strips. Using small strips will create a smoother finish.

4 Leave to dry. Remove the papier-maché bowl by peeling away the cling film and trim round the edge with scissors.

3 Pour some glue into a bowl and add water to dilute it so that it looks like single cream. Dip the newspaper into the glue and start to paste the pieces onto the bowl. Continue to put newspaper onto the bowl, making about 3 layers of paper.

5 Paint the bowl. You may need 2 layers of paint for an even finish, leaving to dry between layers.

6 Cut out flower and leaf shapes from wrapping paper and glue onto the inside and outside of the bowl with undiluted PVA glue. To give the bowl a shiny finish, brush undiluted PVA all over it and leave to dry.

9 PAPIER-MACHÉ MASKS

This is a fun project which even the youngest children can make. Papier maché means "mashed paper" in French and is a great way of transforming bits of old newspaper into all sorts of shapes and decorations. The gluey paste, made from flour and water, is wonderfully tactile and perfectly safe for little people.

Materials
- Bowl and spoon
- Plain flour
- Water
- Newspaper
- Balloon
- Scissors
- White paint and brush
- Felt
- PVA glue
- Felt-tipped pens

1 Make the papier-maché paste by putting some flour in a bowl and adding water to it. Mix it until it has formed a smooth paste with the consistency of thick cream.

2 Tear strips of newspaper. Don't worry if the strips are different sizes.

3 Blow the balloon up and tie a knot. Dip the newspaper strips into the flour paste and lay onto the balloon. Smooth the newspaper pieces slightly and continue until about half of the balloon is covered with paper. Paste about 3 layers of paper in this area. Leave to dry overnight until the paper goes hard.

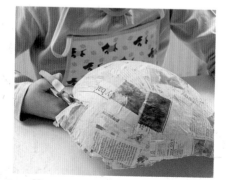

4 Burst the balloon! Trim round the mask with scissors to neaten the edges.

5 Draw 2 eyes onto the mask and cut them out. You may need an adult to help with this.

6 Paint the front of the mask and leave it to dry.

7 Using the templates on page 124, cut out all the features for your mask from felt. Glue them onto the mask and leave to dry.

10 SIMPLE DOLL'S HOUSE

Doll's houses can be very expensive, so make this cute home for your dollies using old boxes and wrapping papers for free. Collect old boxes – shoe boxes, cereal boxes and little sweet boxes are ideal – and decorate them with paint and patterned papers, creating soft furnishings from scraps of fabric for a cosy home that any doll or teddy would be delighted to live in.

Materials
- Shoe box
- Scrap cardboard (old cereal boxes are ideal)
- Wrapping paper
- PVA glue
- Small boxes (sweet packets are good)
- Foil wrappers
- 3 small matchboxes
- Paper clips
- Felt-tipped pens
- Shaped scissors
- Paint and brush
- Scraps of fabric
- Paper cake cases

1 Using a large shoe box as the structure of the house, cut a piece of cereal packet to make the roof of your house. Make it about 2cm (¾ in.) wider than the box and about twice the depth. Cover it in nice paper with glue and fold in half.

2 Apply glue along the front and back of the top of the box and glue the roof in place. Hold it in position until the glue dries.

3 To find the size of the floors measure the width and depth of the shoe box and add 3cm (1¼ in.) to both measurements. Cut out a piece of cardboard to this size. Bend over 1.5cm (½ in.) along both sides and the back, and cut the corners off. Stick a piece of patterned paper onto it and cut along the front with some shaped scissors.

4 Glue along the 2 sides and back of the cardboard and stick inside the house around the middle to form the upper floor.

5 Measure the walls of the house and cut out pieces of wrapping paper to use as wallpaper, gluing them in place.

6 Make a sofa from 2 small boxes glued together with curved pieces of cardboard stuck at each end.

7 When the glue is dry, paint the sofa and decorate with felt-tipped pens.

8 To make a bed, find a thin box and cut a headboard and footboard from cardboard. Glue onto the ends of the box. Paint the bed then make a quilt by decorating a coloured piece of paper with squares of tissue paper.

9 Cut a small box in half and then cut out a square on each side to make a table. Paint and leave to dry.

10 Roll up small pieces of kitchen foil, twist them into shape and glue them onto paper to make picture frames. Draw a picture in the middle and stick on the wall. Twist another piece of foil and form one end into a ball, flattening it to make a lamp stand. Glue a paper cake case to the top as a lampshade.

11 Glue 3 empty matchboxes together and cover in a piece of wrapping paper. Cut a small slit in the front of each drawer and push a paper clip through to make handles.

12 Place the items into the doll's house to make it look like a home.

11 TISSUE-PAPER FLOWERS

Materials
- Tissue paper in different colours
- Twigs
- Pipe cleaners
- Scissors
- Ruler

Have flowers all year round with these wonderful tissue-paper blooms that will never wilt or fade. They are very easy to make and would make a great gift for grannies and aunts, or a perfect Mother's Day present. Collect tissue paper from presents and packaging or buy some from card and stationery shops using several colours in each flower, and fasten onto a twig using a pipe cleaner.

1 Measure and cut 10 pieces of tissue paper 24cm x 30cm (9½in. x 12in.). Lay them on top of each other.

2 Fold all the layers of paper over by about 3cm (1¼in.) and make a crease.

3 Continue to fold the paper until the whole thing resembles a concertina.

4 Cut both ends of the strip into either a curved petal shape or thin strips using the scissors.

5 Take a large pipe cleaner and twist it around the middle of the paper strips.

6 Carefully pull each layer of paper out to form the petals.

7 Twist the pipe cleaner onto the end of a twig. Add a leaf shape if you like. Make a few flowers in different colours to create a beautiful bouquet.

12 CARDBOARD SANDALS

Design and make your own shoes using materials that would normally be thrown away. When making these sandals, look for brightly coloured cereal boxes to use for the straps and decorations and collect corrugated cardboard (shops are often a good source for empty boxes) for the soles. Make sure that the cardboard you use for the soles is not shiny so that they will not be slippy.

Materials
- Empty cereal boxes
- Corrugated cardboard box
- Scissors
- Pen
- PVA glue

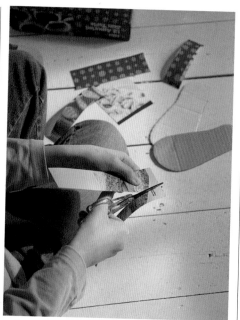

1 Put your foot onto a piece of the corrugated cardboard box and draw round it. Ask someone to help you if necessary!

2 Cut the 2 feet shapes out. Draw round these shapes and cut out another 2 soles from the corrugated cardboard. Cut 2 strips of card from a cereal packet and lay them over the top of your feet to check that they will be long enough for the strap. Add 5cm (2in.) to this.

3 Bend each end under 2.5cm (1in.) and glue it to the top of 1 of the soles. Glue the second soles onto the top of the first one and leave to dry.

4 Cut out a number of colourful shapes from old cardboard food packets to make flower decorations. Cut one piece with curves to make the petals and a smaller round piece for the centre.

5 To finish the sandals glue the shapes onto the straps.

RECYCLING

13 CORK ANIMALS

Collect a pile of corks and create a whole jungle of these cute animals. Ask an adult to cut the corks for you (a bread knife works very well) and then stick them together, using the little bits left over to make the ears, eyes and horns. Ask friends to save corks for you so that you can make lots of animals. You can also buy them from home-brewing shops if you have difficulty getting hold of them.

Materials
- Corks
- PVA glue
- Bread knife
- Scissors
- Yellow and brown wool
- Small beads for eyes

1 To make the giraffe, take 7 corks and cut 4 of them as shown above. Glue them together to make the giraffe shape. Leave to dry before moving.

2 Cut some little strands of brown wool and glue them down the back of the giraffe's neck to make a mane. Cut a short length, fold it in half, knot it at the end and stick on the back to form a tail. Cut little pieces of cork to make the horns and ears, gluing them in place on the head. Finish with 2 small beads glued on as eyes.

3 To make the lion, take 5 corks and cut them into the shapes shown above. Stick them together to make the lion, leaving aside 1 piece of cork that will become the face. Leave to dry.

4 To make the mane, wind yellow wool a few times around your fingers.

5 Take the wool off your hand and tie another piece of wool around the middle and pull tightly, knotting it in place.

6 Stick the mane onto the back of the lion's head and then stick the piece of cork onto the animal's neck to make the head. Cut out small pieces of cork for the ears and a triangular piece for the nose. Glue in place. Knot a loop of wool for the tail and stick beads on for the eyes.

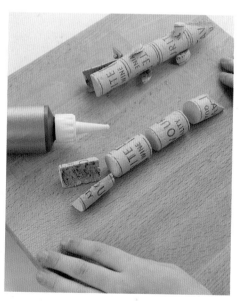

7 To make a crocodile, cut out the corks as shown. Glue them together and leave to dry.

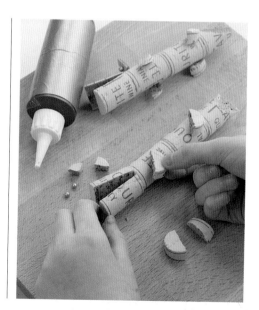

8 Cut half pieces of cork for the legs and glue 4 of them in place. Cut small pieces of cork and glue onto the head, attaching a bead to each to make the eyes.

14 WOVEN PLASTIC-BAG FLAG AND BUNTING

Plastic bags cannot be recycled and can cause real problems in landfill sites, so why not turn them into these fun decorations instead? Use any old bags in bright colours to make bunting, which looks great in the garden and will withstand all weathers. Cut strips of plastic and weave this great flag then find a stick to tie it on, to blow in the wind. Use paper bags or even old magazine pages if you don't want to use plastic.

Materials
- Plastic bags
- Stapler
- Scissors
- Pinking shears
- Felt-tipped pen
- Glue stick
- Twig
- Ribbon

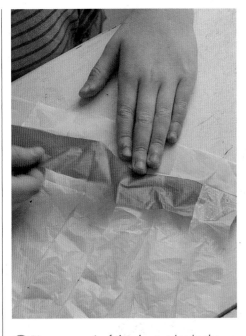

1 To make the flag, start by cutting strips of plastic bags about 2.5cm (1in.) wide. Cut 9 strips of one colour measuring about 45cm (18in.) for the horizontal strips and then cut 12 strips in two colours measuring 30cm (12in.) for the vertical strips. You can use a ruler if you like although it doesn't matter if they are not very accurate.

2 Take a short strip and glue the 9 long strips onto it alternating from front to back sticking 1 strip on the top and the next one on the underside of the short strip.

3 Now weave 1 of the short strips in the second colour through the long strips, gluing both ends to the long strips to hold them in place.

4 Continue to weave the short strips through the long strips alternating the colours until you have made the flag. Glue all the ends of the strips in place.

5 Cut out a star shape from another plastic bag and glue it onto the middle of the flag with PVA glue.

6 Cut 2 strips of plastic bag and fold them in half and staple 1 at the top of the flag along one side and the other at the bottom on the same side to make ties. Tie these onto a stick or twig to make your flag pole.

For the Bunting

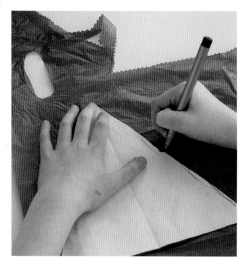

1 Cut out a triangle of paper to use as a pattern. Draw around it onto plastic bags with a felt-tipped pen.

2 Cut out the triangles using pinking shears so that they have a nice patterned edge. Don't worry if you don't have any pinking shears, as ordinary scissors will be fine.

3 Staple the triangles onto a length of ribbon, making it as long as you like. Use the ends of the ribbon to tie the bunting in place.

15 JUGGLING ANIMALS

Have hours of fun with these great juggling balls which have been made into the shapes of animals. Use scraps of fabric and felt to make a rabbit, a mouse, a chicken and a dog, filling them with dried lentils or dried peas, which make them just the right weight for perfect juggling – with practice of course!

Materials
- Fabric
- Felt
- Lentils or dried peas
- Spoon
- Needle and thread

1 Cut out a piece of paper 14cm (5½ in.) square and then use this as a template to cut out 2 squares of fabric for each animal. Use a variety of designs to make up a set.

2 Using the templates on page 124, cut out the features needed for each animal from paper. Pin the shapes onto felt and cut around them with scissors.

3 Place the fabric squares with right sides together, carefully positioning the felt decorations inside so that they just cross the edge of the fabric. Stitch around the 3 sides of the fabric, making the stitches small enough that the lentils will not fall out between them.

4 Turn the fabric bag the right way out. Check that the felt decorations are securely stitched in place.

5 Fill the bag about ¾ full of lentils or dried peas.

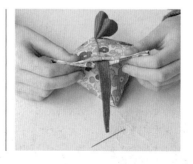

6 To finish the beanbag, stitch closed the remaining open side, lining up the stitched seams together, and pushing the end of a tail into the stitching. Finish the stitching with a few small stitches to secure the thread firmly.

16 POTATO AND APPLE PRINT T-SHIRTS

Potato printing is a traditional technique that can be used to decorate all sorts of things from plain T-shirts and bags to plain paper and card as well as to make gift papers and greetings cards. Using cookie cutters is an easy way to create your shape and requires little cutting. Apple printing is even easier – just cut the apple in half and print away! Make sure that you use fabric paints if the finished item is to be washed.

Materials
- Potatoes
- Apples
- T-shirts
- Potato cutters
- Knife
- Fabric paints
- Paper plates
- Kitchen roll
- Buttons
- Ribbon

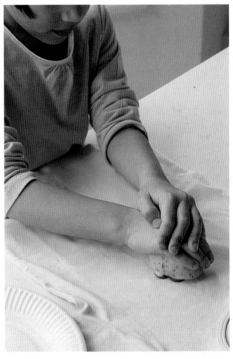

1 To print with potatoes, ask an adult to cut a potato in half. Push a cutter into the cut side. Cut round the edge of the cutter and then remove it leaving the raised shape. Dry the surface of the potato with kitchen roll.

2 Put some fabric paint onto a plate and dip the potato shape into it. Press it lightly onto scrap paper to remove any excess paint.

3 Press the potato onto a T-shirt in the desired position. Press down firmly for even printing. Remove the potato carefully making sure that the paint does not smudge. Dab off any remaining paint from the potato.

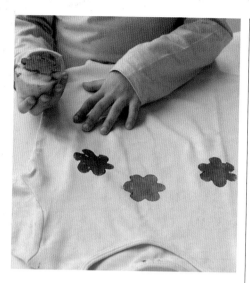

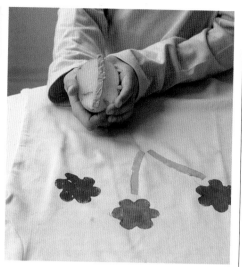

4 Repeat the process using different colours of fabric paint.

5 Using the other half of the potato ask an adult to help cut a stalk shape. Dip the stalk shape in green paint and print stalks onto the T-shirt. Leave to dry.

6 Follow the manufacturer's instructions on the fabric paint and iron the T-shirt (if necessary) to fix the paint. Sew buttons onto the centre of the flowers and a small ribbon bow at the base of the bunch of flowers.

7 For apple printing, first ask an adult for help cutting an apple in half. Remove the stalk and blot the surface dry using kitchen roll. Put fabric paint onto a plate and place the cut apple in it. Press lightly onto a scrap of paper to blot off any excess paint.

8 Press the apple firmly onto the T-shirt. Carefully remove the apple and wipe the remaining paint off with kitchen roll.

9 Dip the apple in another colour of paint and print an apple shape on either side of the first.

10 Using a potato, cut a leaf shape and a small stalk shape. Print a leaf onto the middle apple and a stalk (using brown paint or a mixture of a little red and a little green paint together) onto each apple. Leave to dry and then follow the instructions for the fabric paint to fix the printed paint.

17 MOBILE

Make a mobile as a lovely decoration for your bedroom. Cut out circles of paper, using old magazines or wrapping paper and stick them together, threading a length of wool through the middle of them, then tie the decorations onto a twig or branch. Hang your mobile above your bed so that you can watch it while you doze.

Materials
- Old magazines
- Scrap of cardboard
- Something round to draw round to make a template (2 sizes)
- Pen
- Scissors
- Wool
- Twig

RECYCLING

1 Draw 2 circles of different sizes using any round object on a sheet of cardboard and cut them out. We used a glass for the large circle and a small jar for the smaller one. Cut out 1 circle in each size.

2 Draw round the circles on pictures in an old magazine, looking for nice colours, funny images or interesting shapes, and cut them out.

3 Fold 2 of the circles cut out of the magazines in half and glue them together.

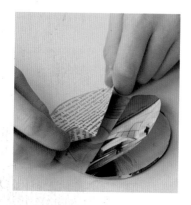

4 Open out 1 side of the pair of circles. Fold a third circle in half and glue 1 side of it down next to the first folded circle. Repeat until you have lots of groups of small and large circles.

5 Take a length of wool and lay it between the 2 open semicircles of paper. Glue one semicircle and press the other down so that the wool is stuck along the centre. Glue more circles onto each length of wool until you have about 6 on each strand. Make 4 lengths in all.

6 Take the twig and tie the lengths of wool onto it – 1 at each end and 2 evenly spaced in the middle. Tie the strands with a double knot to hold them in place.

7 Tie a final length of wool onto the twig in two places to make the hanger.

18 FELT BEADS

These colourful beads are made from pieces of felt rolled up together into a sausage shape, glued and then cut into slices. Play around with different colour combinations and then thread them onto some cord to make fun necklaces and bracelets.

Materials
- Felt sheets
- PVA glue
- Scissors
- Ruler
- Needle and embroidery thread

1 Cut out a rectangle of felt measuring 12cm x 10cm (5in. x 4in.). Cut another rectangle in another colour measuring 12cm x 8cm (5in. x 3in.)

2 Lay the smaller rectangle onto the larger one matching the 12cm (5in.) width and leaving a small gap at both ends. Paste glue along the edge.

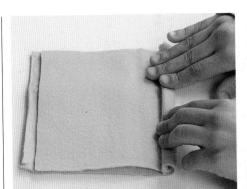

3 Roll up the felt from the glued edge.

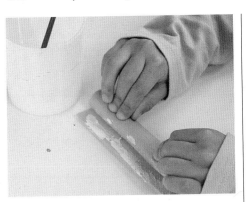

4 Paste glue along the remaining edge and stick the roll together, holding it in place until the glue dries. Hold in place with elastic bands if you like until the glue dries.

5 When the glue is completely dry, cut the felt roll into beads, making each one about 2cm (¾in.) wide using the scissors. Repeat these steps with different coloured felts to make a selection of colourful beads.

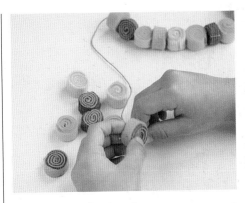

6 Thread the beads onto the thread with a needle to make a necklace. Try not to put beads of the same colour next to each other. Tie the thread into a knot to finish.

19 FELTED BAG

Felt is a really easy fabric to use as it doesn't need hemming. To make your own, put an old wool jumper (check with an adult first!) in a washing machine at a temperature of about 70 degrees and, hey presto, when the jumper dries it will have shrunk and become felted, ready for you to turn into something else.

Materials
- Wool jumper
- Washing machine!
- Scissors
- Large button
- Wool
- Needle and thread
- Paper to make a template

1 Wash the jumper in the washing machine at 70 degrees to felt it. Let it dry then cut out a rectangle measuring 20cm x 24cm (8in. x 9½in.) and fold in half.

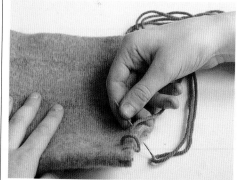

2 Thread wool through a needle and tie a knot in the end. Stitch along both sides of the bag and finish with a knot at each side.

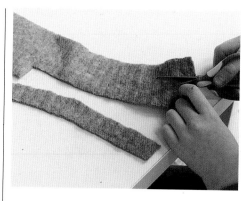

3 Cut 2 straps from the jumper. We used the ribbing at the bottom of the jumper. Make the straps about 2.5cm (1in.) wide and about 20cm (8in.) long.

4 Stitch each end onto the bag with 4 big stitches.

5 Using the template on page 125, cut out a paper flower shape. Pin onto the felted wool and cut out 2 flower shapes. We cut 1 from the ribbing and 1 from the main jumper so that we had two different colours.

6 Stitch the 2 flowers on top of each other with wool and then sew a button at the centre, stitching the whole thing to the bag with a needle and thread.

20 T-SHIRT HAND PUPPETS

Recycle old T-shirts and make them into these sweet hand and finger puppets which are lots of fun to play with. Save T-shirts that you have grown out of (patterned shirts work really well) and cut them up using the template at the back of the book. T-shirt fabric is very easy to sew and the great thing about it is that it does not fray.

Materials
- Old T-shirts
- Paper for pattern
- Scissors
- Pins
- Needle and thread
- Stuffing
- Ric rac braid
- PVA glue

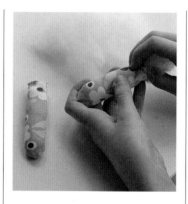

1 Using the template on page 126, cut out a paper pattern for the hand puppet, ear and leg. Lay the patterns onto a double thickness of T-shirt fabric. Pin in place and cut out 2 pieces for the puppet, 4 pieces for the ears and 4 pieces for the legs.

2 With the right sides of the fabric together, pin and stitch the ears together using a small running stitch. Turn them inside out so that the patterned side of the fabric is showing and fill them with stuffing then sew them closed.

3 With right sides of the fabric together, pin the 2 pieces for the hand puppet together, positioning the ears at the top of the head between the 2 pieces, with the raw edges matching. Stitch all the way round the edge of the puppet.

4 Sew the legs together as with the ears, turn the right way out and stuff. Stitch the legs in place and glue ric rac braid round the bottom of the body.

5 Cut out a nose from felt and glue onto the face. Sew buttons on for the eyes and stitch a bow at the neck or onto one of the ears.

To make finger puppets, cut out a front and back piece as for the ears of the hand puppet and with right sides together, stitch all the way round leaving an opening at the bottom. Turn the right way out. Cut out ears and a face from felt and glue in place.

NATURAL

21 EGGSHELL MOSAIC MIRROR

The earliest mosaics are thousands of years old and show beautiful pictures made from fragments of pottery. Try making one at home using eggshells coloured with food dyes. Break them into small pieces to create an all-over pattern or just a simple border for a mirror.

Materials
- Eggshells
- Mirror
- Scrap paper and tape
- Paint and brush
- Food colouring
- Bowls
- Water
- Kitchen roll
- PVA glue

1 Wash the eggshells thoroughly. Pour water into the bowls and put a few drops of food colouring in each. The more food colouring that you use, the stronger the colour of the finished eggs will be. Put the eggshells into the coloured water.

2 Leave the eggshells in the coloured water for at least 1 hour. Take them out and if you would like a stronger colour, pop them back into the water for a while. When you are happy with the colours, remove the eggshells and rinse them under the tap. Leave to dry on kitchen roll.

3 Break up the coloured eggshells into smallish pieces. Keep the different colours separate.

4 Paint the frame of a mirror, covering the glass with scrap paper held in place with tape so that it will not get paint on it. Leave to dry and then apply a second coat if the first is streaky.

5 Put PVA glue onto the frame and stick the small pieces of eggshell onto it. We made a border around the edge of the frame and the mirror, a leaf shape at each corner and a wavy line along each side, but you can make up any pattern you like. Cover the whole frame with eggshells or just make smaller patterns. When you have finished, remove the scrap paper from the mirror.

22 WALNUT BABIES

You'll go nuts over these sweet walnut babies. Halves of walnut shells have been turned into cute cradles for the babies made from wooden beads, decorated with bits of ribbon and fabric. Walnut shells are easy to split but ask an adult to do it for you. Make a walnut mummy to look after your brood, by adding an apron and headscarf to an upright whole nut.

Materials
- Walnut halves (they are easy to split but ask an adult for help)
- Wooden beads
- Stuffing
- Scissors
- Scraps of fabric
- Ric rac braid
- Ribbon
- Felt-tipped pens
- PVA glue

1 Ask an adult for some help breaking a walnut in two, then remove the nut from inside. Take a small piece of stuffing or cotton wool and roll it into a ball shape. Apply a dab of glue inside one of the walnut half and push the stuffing inside.

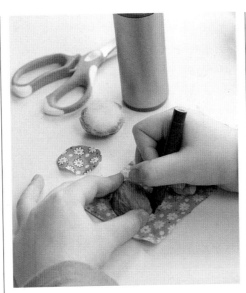

2 Lay a walnut half flat side down onto the fabric and draw round it with a pen. Cut out the oval shape with a pair of scissors. Paste a small amount of glue around the edge of the nutshell and stick the fabric in place.

3 Glue a short length of ric rac braid round the edge of the nutshell, starting and finishing at one end.

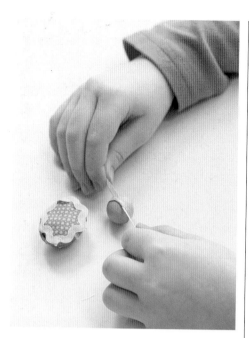

4 To make the baby's head, tie a piece of ribbon around a bead, using a little dab of glue to hold it in place. Tie into a bow and trim the ends short.

5 Draw a face onto the bead with coloured felt-tipped pens, marking semi-circles for the closed eyes of sleeping babies and dots for the open eyes of awake babies.

6 Fix the head onto the nutshell with a spot of glue. You could also add a ribbon underneath the head as a decoration.

7 To make a walnut mum use a whole walnut. Cut a small apron from fabric and glue it onto the nut with a short length of ribbon. Cut a small triangle of fabric and glue it onto the bead to make a headscarf then glue the bead onto the walnut.

23 PINECONE ANIMALS

Next time you go for a walk in the countryside or park, look out for pinecones, twigs, leaves, seeds and other things that could be used to make funny creatures like these. Make sure that you only take things from the ground (don't pick things from trees) and avoid picking berries as they can often be poisonous.

Materials
- Pinecones
- Twigs
- Seed pods
- Rose hips
- Bits of foliage
- Seeds
- Star anise
- PVA glue

NATURAL

1 Use twigs as legs for your pinecone animal. Choose little twigs of similar length and put a dab of glue onto one end of each. Push into the cone and leave to dry. Glue a pinecone or seed head on top to make the head. Try using twigs or little pinecones for antlers, either pushing them in place or gluing them in position.

2 Collect feathers to make little birdie creatures. Push them into seed heads and make a face using seeds from various trees and plants as the eyes and beak.

3 Rose hips are great for eyes. Dab glue onto the tips of them and push them into the pinecone. Little pinecones can be used for noses (among other things!). Glue one onto a larger pinecone.

4 Little sprigs of foliage make good ears, antlers, arms and anything else that you can think of. Cut little pieces from rosemary, lavender or other shrubs and trees and glue them to hold them in position.

5 To make an owl first glue pumpkin seeds around the top of a pinecone. Star anise are perfect for the owl's eyes and long seeds fixed in place with glue can be used to make the beak and claws. Sprigs of foliage pushed into the pinecone finish off the owl.

6 Create little pinecone people using pom-pom seed heads, seeds and twigs. Try to use the natural properties of the things that you collect. Here the stalk which is in thin strands makes perfect hair for your person.

24 PUMPKIN ANIMALS

Carving pumpkins for Halloween is great fun but can be difficult for younger children. These pumpkin creatures are made by simply sticking vegetables and seeds into the pumpkin and squash, without needing to use a sharp knife. All sorts of funny faces and bodies can be created, and when you have finished playing, you can cook and eat the pumpkins for a delicious supper.

Materials

- Pumpkins and squash in any shape, size and colour
- Selection of other vegetables – carrots, sprouts, aubergines and courgettes are all great
- Pumpkin and sunflower seeds, fresh ginger, bay leaves
- Cocktail sticks
- Wooden skewers

1 Lay all your vegetables out on the table so that you can see what you have got.

2 Play around with different arrangements to create some crazy creatures!

3 Push one end of a cocktail stick into the vegetable that you would like to use and then push the other end into your pumpkin. Push seeds into pumpkins to make eyebrows, teeth, noses etc.

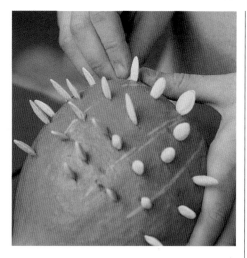

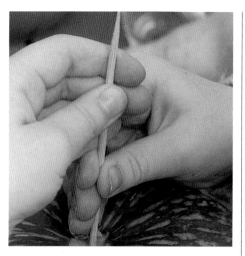

4 Seeds make great spikes for hedgehogs. Push them into a squash, using the pointed top of the squash as a nose. Slices of vegetables become eyes when held in place with cocktail sticks.

5 Push half of one of the wooden skewers into a squash to join one onto the other. Ask an adult to help if the skin of the squash is very tough.

6 Push another squash onto the rest of the skewer to join two together.

7 Make antlers, ears, arms, eyes by attaching them to the squash with cocktail sticks.

8 Bay leaves are a good shape to use as hair or headdresses and decoration on your creatures. It is easy to push cocktail sticks through them, which can then be pushed into the pumpkins.

25 DRIED-FLOWER FAIRIES

Pressing flowers is a craft that dates back to the nineteenth century and is still popular today. Make sure that you have permission to pick flowers and then put them in a flower press or between the pages of a heavy book or telephone directory for about a week. When the blooms have dried out and are nice and flat, use them to create all sorts of pictures, like these pretty flower fairies that can be made into cards or put in frames to give as gifts.

Materials
- Fresh flowers
- Flower press or pile of heavy books
- Glue stick
- Coloured paper
- Cream card
- Coloured card
- Scissors
- Pencil and ruler

1 Collect fresh flowers and lay carefully between 2 sheets of paper in the flower press. Tighten the flower press up and leave for at least a week.

2 Using the template on page 126, cut out a fairy shape then draw round it onto plain coloured paper and cut it out.

3 Stick it on to a piece of cream card about 15cm (6in.) by 10cm (4in.), adding a piece of paper for the fairy's hair.

4 Open the flower press and carefully remove the flowers. Arrange them on the paper fairy to make a pretty dress and hat. When you are happy with the arrangement, carefully lift each flower or petal and dab some glue onto the paper and press the petal or flower down gently to stick it in place.

5 Cut a piece of coloured card 17.5cm (7in.) by 12.5cm (5in.) and fold in half. Glue the flower fairy onto the front of it, making an even border all the way round.

26 PAINTED STONES

Look for pebbles and stones in the shape of houses with a flat bottom and round top and paint them to look like cute cottages. Bear in mind that some beaches do not allow you to remove stones so check before you take any. Try and buy some at a garden centre if you can't get hold of any at the seaside.

Materials
- Stones in various sizes with a flattish bottom
- Paints
- Paintbrushes
- PVA glue
- Twig

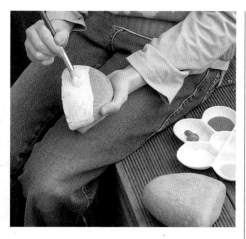

1 Paint the bottom half of a large stone white to make the walls of the house. Leave to dry. Then, if you can still see the stone through the paint, cover it again with another coat.

2 Paint the roof using a darker colour – usually orange or brown though you can try any other you particularly like – and again leave to dry.

3 Paint a door, windows and flowers onto the stone using a variety of colours. Paint tiles onto the roof or texture it to look like thatch and also paint plants growing up the walls.

4 When the paint is completely dry, you can cover the stone with PVA glue to make it shiny.

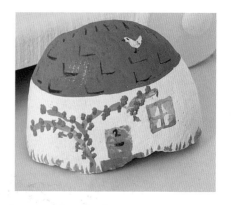

27 DRIFTWOOD GAME

This great game is perfect for the beach or the park. Simply collect 4 driftwood sticks of a similar length and bind them together to make the board. Tie small sticks together to make the crosses and collect pebbles or shells for the noughts. The aim of the game is to make a line of 3 noughts or crosses, while trying to block your opponent from doing the same. The first player to get 3 in a row wins.

Materials
- 4 sticks about 40cm (16in) long
- 10 short, thin sticks
- Raffia (or string)
- 5 pebbles
- Scissors

1 Find 4 sticks that are about the same length and arrange them in a criss-cross pattern. Take a piece of raffia and wind it a couple of times round the join of 2 sticks, tying them with a knot.

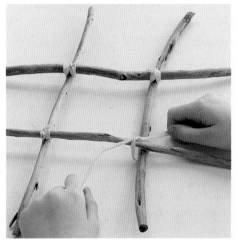

2 Continue to bind all the sticks together in the same way.

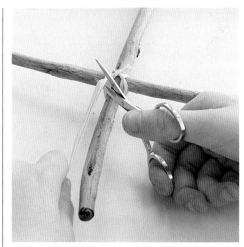

3 Use a pair of scissors to trim the ends of the raffia.

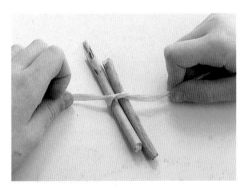

4 Snap thinner lengths of stick into 10 short pieces. Make 5 crosses by taking two sticks and tying raffia around the middle of them.

5 Twist 1 stick to form a cross shape and tie the raffia across the other way to hold it in place, finishing with a knot. Trim off the ends of the raffia with scissors.

28 DRIFTWOOD BOATS

Collect driftwood from the beach to make these little boats and have hours of fun sailing them in rock pools or back home in the bath! Build up a fleet using a variety of shapes of wood, adding different triangles of fabric or paper for the sails. These boats are so simple to make, even the youngest of beachcombers will be able to create them.

Materials
- Driftwood
- Sticks
- Plasticine
- Scraps of fabric
- Paper
- Felt-tipped pen
- Pinking shears
- PVA glue

1 Draw a triangle on paper and cut it out to use as a pattern. Lay it down on the fabric and draw round it with a felt-tipped pen.

2 Cut the fabric triangles out using the pinking shears. Use normal scissors if you don't have any.

3 Apply a line of glue down the centre of the front side of each triangle.

4 Fix a stick onto the line of glue on the sail to make the mast and leave it to dry for a few minutes.

5 Take a piece of plasticine and stick it in the middle of the driftwood boat. Push the mast into the plasticine to make a sail.

FABRIC

29 GLOVE CREATURES

These woolly creatures are so easy to create you won't need to knit a stitch to make them. Find an old glove – this project is perfect for people who often lose one – fold in some of the fingers and stuff it with padding. Make a funny face by sewing buttons and scraps of braid onto your creation, or use felt and glue if you prefer.

Materials
- Old gloves
- Needle and thread
- Stuffing
- Buttons, braids, ribbons and pom-pom

1 Fold the thumb and the two middle fingers that are not needed for ears inside the glove and sew across the openings with a needle and thread.

2 Stuff the glove to make your creature, filling the ears if you want them to stand up, leaving them empty if they are to be folded over.

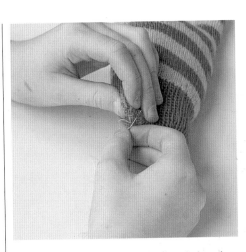

3 Stitch the opening for the hand closed.

4 Make the faces by sewing buttons and pieces of braid and pom poms onto the front of the creature. Stitch the ears down to make the dog. Make the cat in the same way but fold back half of the fingers that make the ears and stitch the openings closed.

30 FABRIC FLOWER BROOCH

This sweet flower brooch is made from scraps of fabric and is very easy to create. It would make a lovely present for friends or family or, alternatively, make one for yourself to wear as a brooch or use as a pretty decoration for a hair band or hat.

Materials
- Scraps of fabric
- Stuffing
- Button
- Safety pin
- Embroidery thread and needle
- Pinking shears
- Paper for pattern

1 Using the designs on page 125 make up 2 templates that you can cut around. Pin them onto a piece of fabric and cut out 2 flower shapes.

2 Stitch the flower shapes together with wrong sides of the fabric together. Use a running stitch all the way round the petals, leaving a small opening.

3 Stuff the flower lightly then continue to stitch around the petal until you have sewn all the way round.

4 Cut out 2 circles of fabric with pinking shears with a diameter of about 4cm (1½ in). Stitch these together as you did with the flower.

5 Stitch the circle to the middle of the flower and then sew a button onto the middle.

6 Using cotton thread and needle, stitch a safety pin to the back of the brooch, finishing with a few small stitches to secure it in place.

31 POM-POM CATERPILLAR

Go pom-pom crazy and make this cute caterpillar. Make pom-poms using wool in shades of green like this one, or go multi-coloured, using oddments of yarn in as many bright colours as you can find. You can buy plastic pom-pom rings from craft shops, but why buy them when you can make them yourself by recycling the cardboard from old cereal boxes?

Materials
- Oddments of wool
- Cardboard
- Pencil and compass
- Large needle
- Scissors
- Felt in white and brown
- PVA glue

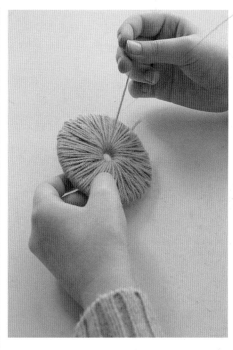

1 Set a compass and pencil to a length of 4cm (1½in) and draw 2 circles next to each other – these will have a diameter of 8cm (3in). Reset the compass to a length of 1cm (½in) and draw a smaller circle in the centre of both. Cut out the cardboard around the outer circles then remove the centres by cutting around the inner circles.

2 Put the two cardboard circles together and start to wind the wool around them, pulling it tightly through the hole in the middle.

3 Continue to wind the wool around the cardboard ring. To make a really dense pom-pom, continue winding the wool over itself until the centre hole is completely full. Leaving a small hole in the centre will make a looser pom-pom.

4 With a pair of scissors, carefully start to cut around the edge of the woolly circle, pushing the blade of the scissors between the two cardboard discs. Cut all the way around.

5 Pull a double length of wool between the cardboard discs and tie it tightly with a knot, leaving a long tail of wool.

6 Carefully pull the cardboard discs off the pom-pom and discard them.

7 Fluff up the pom-pom. Neaten if necessary by trimming the ends of the wool until they form a regular shape.

8 Make 7 pom-poms in total varying the sizes as you prefer. For the head you can make a pom pom using cardboard discs 12cm (5in) across, made with a compass set at 6cm (2.5in). Thread a large needle with the double length of wool, knotted at one end, and push the needle through the middle of each pom-pom to make a caterpillar, leaving it threaded through the head.

9 Make a small red pom-pom using cardboard discs measuring 5cm (2in) in diameter. Thread the needle through it and push it onto the caterpillar to form the nose. Thread the needle back through the nose and head and hold it in place with a knot.

10 Take 3 pieces of wool about 25cm (10in) long and tie into a knot at one end. Braid the 3 lengths together and tie the other end in a knot.

11 Stitch the braids to the top of the head as antennae and then cut 2 circles from felt and stick them onto slightly larger white circles. Glue them onto the face as eyes.

32 FRIENDSHIP BRACELETS

These braided bracelets are so easy and quick to make that you will be creating them for all your friends in no time. Any wool or braid can be used but bear in mind that the chunkier the wool, the thicker the bracelet will be. Experiment with different colour combinations to make great gifts for friends.

Materials
- 2 colours of wool
- Bulldog clip
- Cardboard
- Scissors
- Beads (optional)

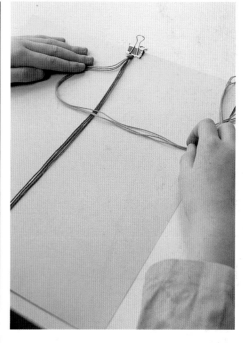

1 Cut 3 70cm (27in) lengths of 2 colours of wool that you think will look good when plaited together. Here turquoise and purple have been used.

2 Put all 6 lengths of wool together and tie them in a simple knot about 5cm (2in) from one end.

3 Hold the knotted end of the wool in place by clipping it to the top of a piece of cardboard or a book. Separate the strands into their different colours then take the left-hand bundle (3 lengths of one colour) and loop it over the right-hand bundle.

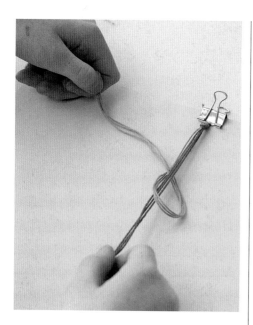

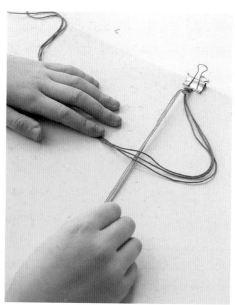

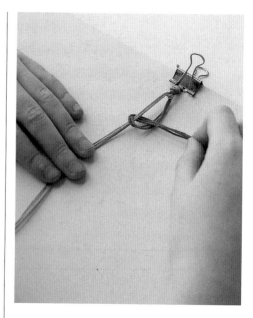

4 Pull the left-hand strands back through the loop and tighten into a knot that sits right against your original knot, all the while holding the right-hand bundle straight.

5 Now straighten the left-hand bundle and loop the right-hand bundle over it.

6 Pull it back through the loop that you have just made and tighten, using exactly the same movement as before just in reverse, again holding the other wool strands straight.

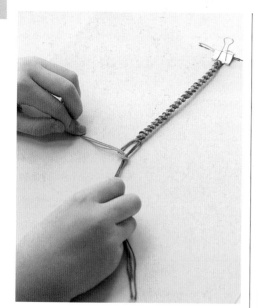

7 Continue to follow these steps until you have the right length to fit around your friend's wrist.

8 Unclip the bracelet from the wooden board and tie the ends into a knot. Thread beads onto some of the individual strands for extra decoration if you like, tying the ends of the wool into large knots to hold the beads in place.

33 SAUSAGE DOG DRAUGHT EXCLUDER

Transform an old pair of tights into an adorable sausage dog. Easy to make, it requires very little sewing and can be made by children of any age especially if the eyes and ears are glued on. We used old mittens for ears, but children's socks would work equally well. Use as a draught excluder, or simply snuggle up with your huggable hound!

Materials
- Old pair of woolly tights
- Wool
- Scraps of fabric
- 2 buttons
- Needle and thread
- Stuffing or old socks (clean!)
- Old mittens
- Scissors

1 Cut one of the legs from an old pair of woolly tights as high up as possible with a pair of scissors.

2 Fill the cut leg of the tights with stuffing (or whatever you are using) so that it forms a sausage shape. Leave a bit unstuffed at the end.

3 Cut a length of wool and tie it firmly around the end of the sausage, finishing with a double knot to hold it in place.

4 At the other end, tie another piece of wool around the toe to make a big doggy nose. Again tie a knot to hold the shape in place.

5 Sew an old mitten onto each side of the sausage just above the nose to make the dog's ears.

6 Make a heart shape by using the template on page 126 and use it to cut out some hearts from scraps of fabric.

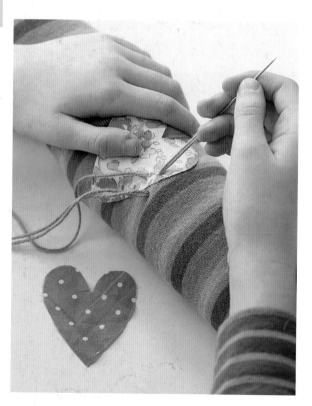

7 Sew the hearts onto the sausage using a needle and wool. Tie a knot in the end of the wool and stitch through the tights. Push the needle up from the back of the heart to the front near the edge and then stitch back through the tights. Continue around each heart shape and finish with a knot.

8 Sew the buttons onto the sausage to make eyes. Tear a strip off some fabric or use a piece of ribbon and tie around the doggy's neck to make his collar.

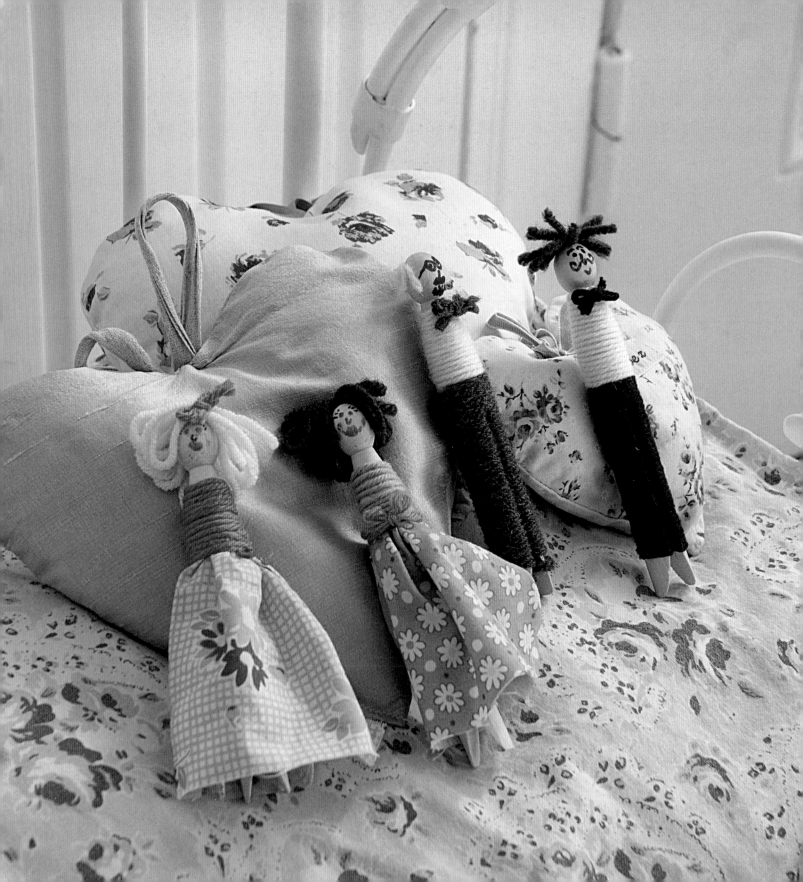

34 PEG DOLLS

Traditional wooden clothes pegs are the perfect size and shape to make into little dolls, dressing them with scraps of fabric and wool. Create different styles of clothing to give your dolls real character, adding bits of ribbon or buttons for extra decoration, and create some men to go with the prettily dressed women. The doll's house on page 43 would make a lovely home for a family of peg dolls.

The doll's house on page 43 would make a lovely home for a family of peg dolls.

Materials
- Clothes pegs
- Felt-tipped pens
- Scraps of fabric
- Wool
- PVA glue
- Scissors

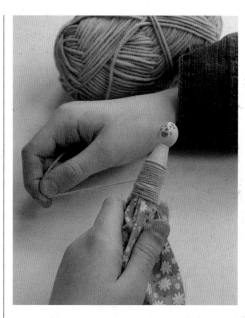

1 Using the felt-tipped pens, draw faces onto the pegs, with the 2 prongs of the peg positioned so that they look like legs.

2 To dress the female dolls measure and cut out a rectangle of fabric about 8cm x 20cm (3in x 8in). Put it around the peg gathering it to make a skirt. Tie a length of wool around the top of it to hold it in place and fasten with a knot.

3 Wrap the wool round the peg from the top of the skirt up to near the head and secure in place at the back with a dab of glue. You may need to hold the wool in place until the glue is dry.

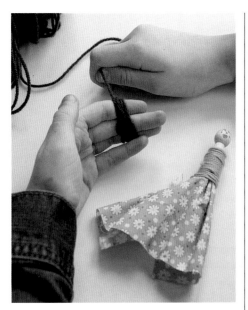

4 To make the hair wrap loops of wool around your fingers.

5 Tie in the middle with a short piece of wool and cut off the ends. Cut open the loops to make the strands of hair.

6 Position the hair on top of the peg so that the face shows and glue it in place.

7 To make the male dolls, wrap the wool from the waist down, again securing the beginning of the wool strand in place with a dab of glue. Wind the wool round the peg and then around just one prong to the foot and cut the wool and glue the end in place. Wrap wool around the other prong, again gluing the beginning and end of the wool.

8 Make the 2 male dolls' hair different by cutting short loops of wool for the first while simply cutting short pieces of wool and glue around the head. Finish by tying bows around the male dolls' necks and around the waist or head of the female dolls.

35 FRENCH KNITTING

Learn how to knit without needles, by French knitting. You will need a knitting "dolly," which you will find in wool and haberdashery shops. Alternatively you can make one yourself using a cotton reel and four pins. The technique looks complicated but is very easy once you get the hang of it, and will produce a knitted tube that you can make into all sorts of things. Make two of these flowers and sew them onto a pair of plain slippers or use one flower as a brooch or decoration for a bag or hat.

● ● ● ● ● ● ● ● ● ● ● ● ● ● ● ● ● ● ● ●

Materials
- Wool in 2 colours
- Wooden cotton reel
- 4 map pins
- Scissors
- Needle to pull the wool over the pins (knitting needle is ideal)
- Button

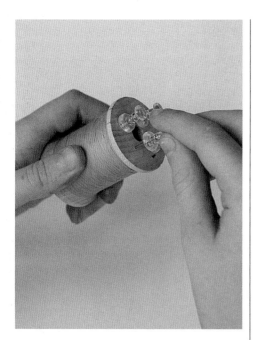

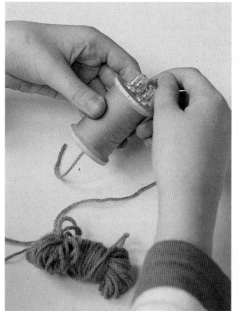

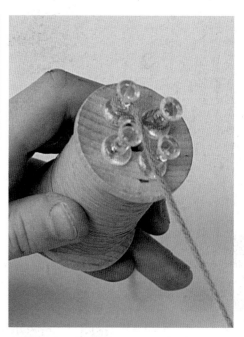

1 To make your French knitting dolly take a wooden cotton reel and push 4 pins into the top, spacing them equally.

2 Take the wool and thread the end of it through the hole in the middle of the bobbin from the top where the pins are to the bottom. When the end comes through the bottom of the bobbin, hold the wool in your left hand.

3 Working in an anti-clockwise direction, loop the wool around each of the 4 pins.

4 Pull the wool around the front of the first pin, above the first loop of wool. Don't loop it around the pin. Slip the knitting needle through the bottom loop, lifting it over the top line of wool and over the top of the pin. Continue by pulling the wool across the front of the next pin above the original wool loop, and loop the bottom loop of wool over the top line and pin. Repeat round each pin, pulling the wool in your left hand slightly through the dolly to pull the knitting through the hole.

5 Continue to knit until you have a length of about 20cm (8in). Keep pulling the knitting through the dolly as you go, being careful not to pull too hard or the knitting will stretch.

6 To finish off the knitting, take a loop on one of the pins onto the knitting needle and loop it over the next pin clockwise. Loop the bottom line of wool on this pin over the top one onto the next pin clockwise. Repeat until only 1 loop of wool remains on only one of the pins. Pull this loop off the pin and thread the wool through, securing it with a knot. Pull the knitting through the dolly and trim the loose ends of wool at each end.

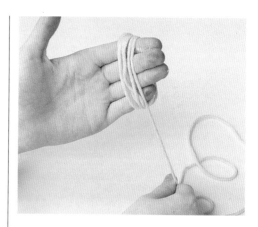

7 Form 5 equal petal shapes with the length of knitting and stitch together at the bottom of each with wool to form the flower shape. Finish with a knot in the wool so that the flower will not come apart.

8 Loop the other coloured wool around your fingers several times. Making lots of loops will create a denser centre for your flower, and making fewer loops will give you a looser centre.

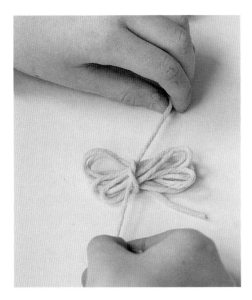

9 Cut the wool and carefully remove it from your fingers. Tie a piece of wool around the centre of the bundle and finish with a knot. Trim the loose ends of the wool.

10 Sew the bundle onto the middle of the knitted flower with a needle and a length of wool then stitch a button onto the centre of that. Sew or glue your flower onto the front of a slipper, making a second one for the other foot!

TEMPLATES

Trace off the templates on the following pages to make up the designs from the projects.

Papier-maché masks

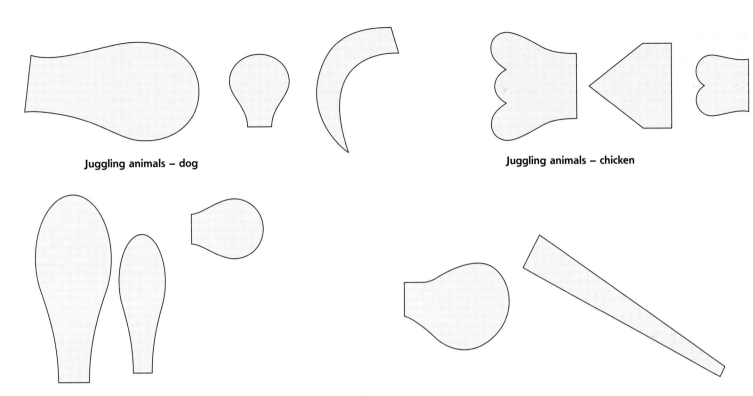

Juggling animals – dog

Juggling animals – chicken

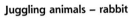

Juggling animals – rabbit

Juggling animals – mouse

Felted bag – flowers

Fabric flower brooch

Dried-flower fairy

T-shirt hand puppets

Sausage dog draught excluder – heart

SUPPLIERS

UK

Early Learning Centre
08705 352 352
www.elc.co.uk

Homecrafts Direct
0116 269 7733
www.homecrafts.co.uk

Hobbycraft
0800 027 2387
www.hobbycraft.co.uk

John Lewis
08456 049 049
www.johnlewis.co.uk

Kidzcraft
01793 327022
www.kidzcraft.co.uk

Paperchase
0161 839 1500 for mail order
www.paperchase.co.uk

Woolworths
0844 811 7111
www.woolworths.co.uk

US

Art Supplies Online
1-800-967-7367
www.artsuppliesonline.com

Craft Site Directory
Useful online resource
www.craftsitedirectory.com

Crafts etc.
1-800-888-0321
www.craftsetc.com

Create For Less
1-866-333-4463
www.createforless.com

Creative Kids Crafts
1-510-364-2369
www.creativekidscrafts.com

Darice
1-866-432-7423
www.darice.com

Hobby Lobby
Stores nationwide
www.hobbylobby.com

Jo-ann Fabric & Crafts
1-888-739-4120
www.joann.com

Kids Craft Supplies
866 777-8654
www.kidscraftsupplies.com

Michaels
Stores nationwide
www.michaels.com

S&S Worldwide Craft Supplies
1-800-288-9941
www.ssww.com

Sunshine Crafts
1-800-729-2878
www.sunshinecrafts.com

Toys "R" Us
Stores nationwide
www.toysrus.com

ACKNOWLEDGEMENTS

I would firstly like to thank Debbie Patterson for the beautiful photography, and whose creativity, eye for detail and inventiveness have helped to make this book. Thank you also to Finn, Ethan and Jed for letting me hijack your mum for several weekends.

A big thank you to our wonderful models: Chloe Allan, Isobel Edwards, Akalia Cox, Amber Seddon, Gracie and Betty Dahl, and Tilda and Erin van Petegem. Your hard work, enthusiasm and patience during photography was fantastic.

Thank you to Robin Gurdon for being a very sensitive and considerate editor and to Liz Sephton for the great design. And many thanks to Cindy Richards, Sally Powell and Pete Jorgensen at CICO for giving me the opportunity to do this book and for the support and organisation offered.

Thank you to Joy and Daniel Dahl for all your help. And thank you to Laurie for everything. This book would not have been possible without the involvement of Gracie and Betty, whose creativity and imagination know no bounds. Thank you lovelies.

INDEX

INDEX

J 745.508/HAR

WALLSEND DISTRICT LIBRARY